Simple and Yummy
Plant Based Recipes

"It's the small moments in life that lead to the great journey. By being present with each bite and moment you can develop beneficial habits that will enable you to live your healthiest journey."

– Cathy XO

Your Food is Ready

All recipes are plant based and gluten free

CATHY BROOKS TRICIA BROOKS

To your healthiest self!

"Change what you consume.

Change your life."

– Tricia XO

Contents

Good Morning and Hello!

Our brains are made up of 73 percent water, and we dehydrate while we sleep.

So drinking water first thing in the morning helps fuel our brain, as hydration is crucial to daily productivity!

It's beneficial to add lemon to your water, which is high in vitamin C. Lemon has a host of antioxidants that help kick the digestion system into action. This wards off infection and boosts your immune system.

Start your day in a healthy way!

P.S. We recommend USDA organic food as a first choice whenever possible.

Green Drink

1/2 cup of micro greens

1 cup of spinach

1 cup of kale

1 cup of arugula (Or three of your favorite dark greens)

1 cup of wild frozen blueberries

1 cup of cherries, mangos or peaches (Your favorite—you choose!)
   We like to add 1 scoop of a greens balance (by Arbonne)

1 cup of water

Blend and enjoy. ***Best to drink immediately.***

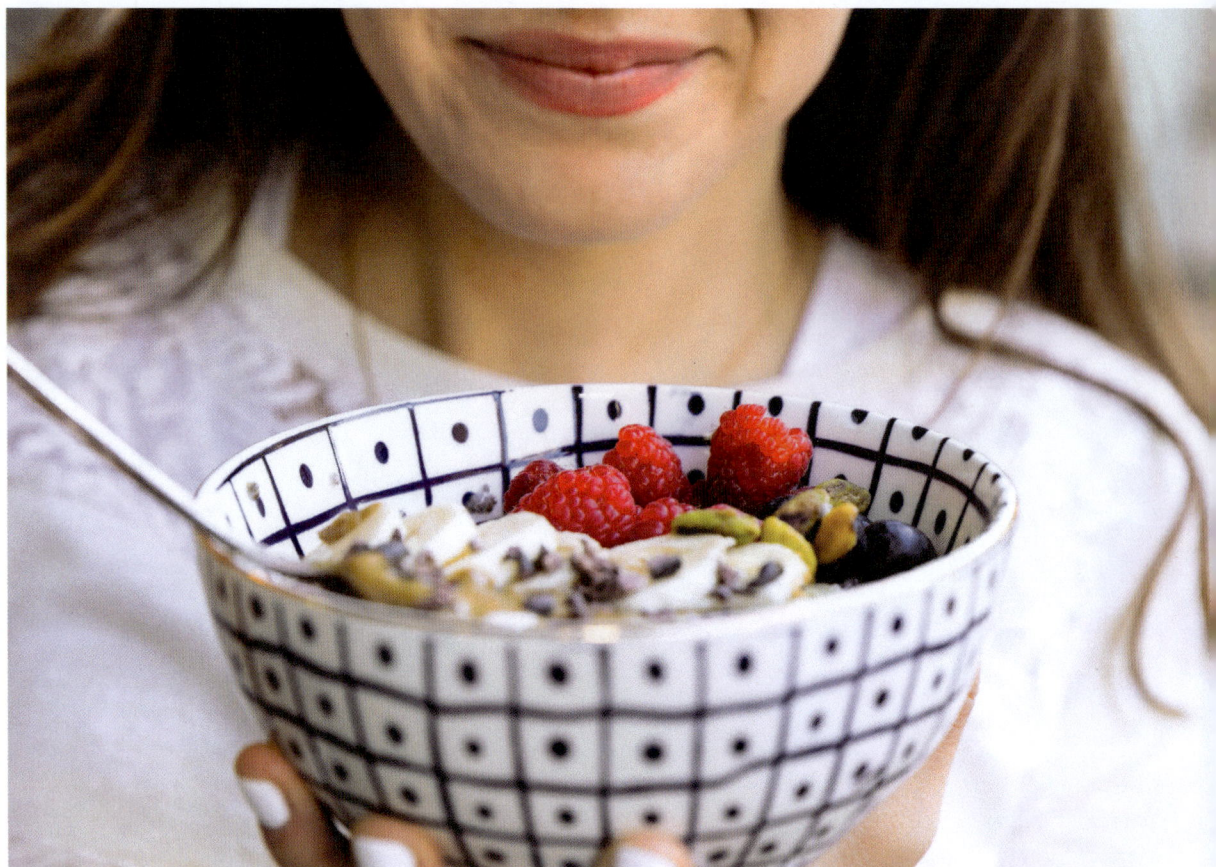

Chia Pot

1/4 cup of soaked chia

1/4 to 1/2 cup of raspberries, blueberries or berries of your choice

2 tablespoons of nut butter

1/4 cup nuts - your choice

1/2 banana sliced

Optional: Cocoa nibs

Fill your bowl with soaked chia and create your pattern with the remaining ingredients. *Have fun and enjoy!*

HOW TO SOAK CHIA

Put 1 cup of plant milk in a container with 1/2 cup chia seeds, and soak it overnight. It will be delicious in the morning!

Chocolate Protein Shakes

Two scoops of chocolate vegan protein powder

Two cups of water or plant based milk

Five to six cubes of ice

One Tablespoon of raw cocoa powder

1/4 of an avocado or 1 tablespoon nut butter

Blend and enjoy!

Garnish: coconut flakes, cocoa nibs and one blueberry just for fun!

Muesli on the go!

MUESLI

1/2 cup gluten free oats

1/2 cup of organic corn flakes

1/4 cup of Raisins or dried fruit of choice

A sprinkle of almonds or nuts of choice

A dash of coconut flakes

Plant based milk

You can always mix the dry contents the night before or week prior and store in an air tight container.

Pour your choice of plant based milk on top, add freshly cut banana if you would like, and enjoy!

Breakfast Protein Burrito

1/2 chopped onion

1/2 teaspoon garlic powder or 1 clove of garlic

1 tablespoon organic triple filtered coconut oil or avocado oil, or water

1/2 cup organic tofu

Two tablespoons of taco seasoning

1/2 cup cooked black or refried beans

Add 1/2 cup of cooked brown rice

Set aside Gluten free tortilla

Breakfast Burrito *continued*

Sauté onion, garlic powder or garlic in a pan with organic triple filtered coconut oil, or avocado oil, or water until almost fully cooked.

Crumble organic tofu and add to the above mixture with the taco seasoning.

Add cooked black or refried beans and brown rice.

Heat and set aside.

GLUTEN FREE TORTILLA

Heat the tortilla in a frying pan.

Put on a plate and then layer the tofu, beans, rice, salsa or cherry tomatoes, avocado and vegan cream cheese (KiteHill plain cream cheese tastes like sour cream. YUM).

NEW POTATOES

1/2 teaspoon rosemary

1/2 teaspoon garlic powder

Cut the new potatoes into wedges and put them in the oven at 250 degrees.

Drizzle coconut oil or avocado oil on top, sprinkle the potatoes with rosemary and garlic powder.

Turn them once to bake them on all sides. Bake for 25 minutes (test with fork).

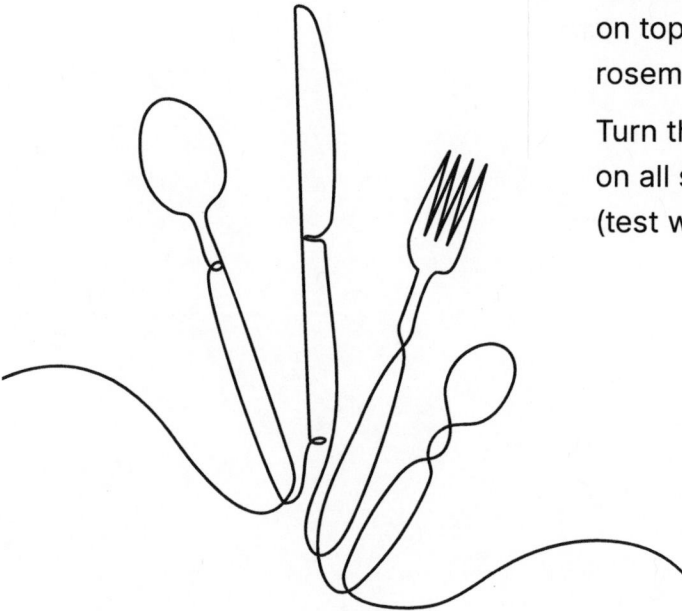

Gluten Free Pesto Pasta

PESTO

4 cups of basil

Half a lemon squeezed

1/4 cup olive oil

Pinch of sea salt

1-2 tablespoons vegan parmesan cheese or nutritional yeast

Blend in Cuisinart or blender until pesto consistency.

Cook gluten free pasta, fold in pesto.

Add raw spinach, pistachios and tomatoes if desired.

Sprinkle with graded plant based parmesan

This Pesto is very rich so a little goes a long way.

Portobello Cauliflower Mash

One portobello per person

1 Tablespoon of coconut oil

1/2 teaspoon Garlic powder

1 head of cauliflower *(serves two-four people)*

Parsley

Plumped sun-dried tomatoes

1-2 tablespoons of Plant butter

Sea salt and pepper for taste

PORTOBELLO MUSHROOMS

One portobello per person

Cut into strips

Sauté in coconut oil with Garlic powder

Set aside

CAULIFLOWER MASH

Cut one head of cauliflower into small pieces

Steam cauliflower al dente
The secret is to not cook it too long - it does not taste as good if it's mushy.

Place cauliflower in the Cuisinart or a blender

Blend until its mashed potato consistency
(add a bit of plant milk if liquid is needed)

Add one or two tablespoons of plant butter into mixture

Salt and pepper to taste

SERVE Immediately

Garnish with portobello mushroom slices, parsley, and plumped sun dried tomatoes if you choose.

*Plumped = Sun dried tomatoes

Polenta Bites

One inch sliced organic polenta per bite

1 teaspoon of organic triple filtered coconut oil

One tablespoon refried beans per bite

1 teaspoon of salsa per bite

One slice of avocado per bite

1/2 teaspoon of chopped cilantro

One lime squeeze

Bed of lettuce

Cut the organic polenta into thick slices

Heat polenta in organic triple filtered coconut oil on the stove top in a pan until warm.

Put polenta pieces on a plate and layer with heated refried beans, salsa, avocado, cilantro, a squeeze of lime and serve on a bed of lettuce.

Yummy Tahini Dressing and Plant Based Ranchish

YUMMY TAHINI DRESSING

3/4 cup of tahini

1/2 of a lemon juiced

1/3 cup of liquid aminos

1/3-1/2 cup of filtered water

1/2 teaspoon garlic powder
or one clove of garlic

Mix in Cuisinart until dressing
consistency

PLANT BASED RANCHISH

6 ounces of firm organic tofu

1/2 of a lemon juiced

1 clove of garlic

2 tablespoons of organic apple cider vinegar

1/2 teaspoon onion granules

1/2 teaspoon mustard powder

1/4 teaspoon sea salt

1/4 cup water

1 Tablespoon chives

2 Tablespoons dill

1 Tablespoon parsley

Mix everything in Cuisinart or blender

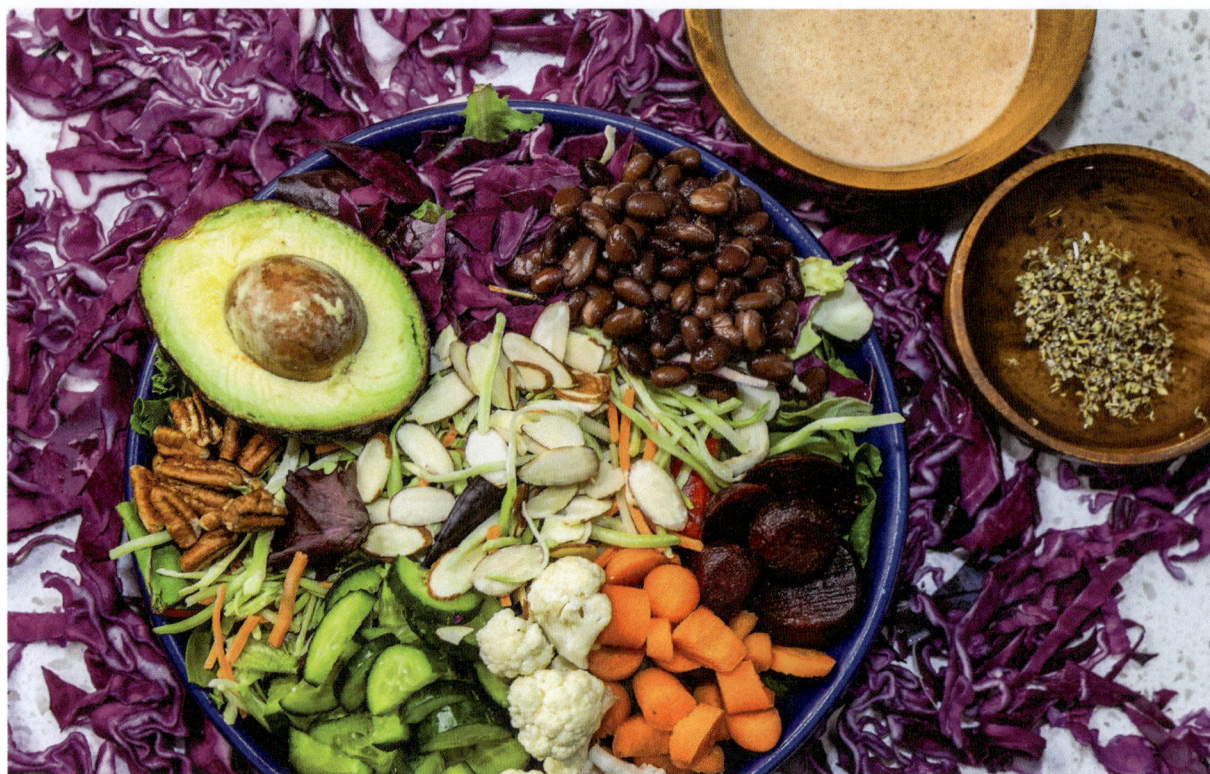

Hey, Gorgeous Salad

Persian cucumbers

Avocado

Carrots

Cauliflower

Black beans

Purple cabbage

Bell peppers

Beets

Pecans

Almonds

Or your favorite vegetables
(*Don't forget to eat the colors of the rainbow*)

Your gut bugs will love you.

Chop up all of the vegetables, place in your desired way and dress.

One could also drizzle extra virgin olive oil, squeezed lemon, basil, oregano and a small amount of powdered garlic for a different flavor.

Enjoy all of this yummy nutrients!

See page 23 for Dressing recipes

Zucchini Zoodles with Tomato Sauce

ZUCCHINI ZOODLES

Spiralized zucchini
(one medium zucchini per person if you are spiraling them yourself)

12 chopped mushrooms

1/2 an onion

2 cups of your favorite spaghetti sauce

1 tablespoon organic triple filtered coconut oil

A dash of water

Vegan parmesan cheese

ZOODLES

Place spiralized zucchini noodles on a plate *(Do not cook the zoodles)*

TOMATO SAUCE

Sauté chopped mushrooms and onion in coconut oil with a dash of water.

Then pour your favorite spaghetti sauce in the pan.

Simmer until its heated

Pour over zoodles and sprinkle vegan parmesan cheese on top!

Bountiful Bowl

1 Carrot

1 beet

2 cups of kale

10 mushrooms

1 carrot

1/2 of a zucchini

Or your favorite vegetables

1/2 a sweet potato

1/4 a cup cooked lentils

1 cup of brown rice

Optional: One tablespoon of organic triple filtered coconut oil if sautéing the vegetables

Precook brown rice, lentils, sweet potato and beets.

Either steam individually or sauté kale, mushrooms, carrot, zucchini, or favorite vegetables.

Layer on top of brown rice and lentils in a bowl.

Pour the Yummy Tahini sauce on top!

See page 23 for Tahini Dressing recipe

A little bit sweeter

Fudgy Balls

One scoop of chocolate vegan protein powder

1 Tablespoon of nut butter

1 teaspoon of chia seeds

1 teaspoon of plant based milk

1 Tablespoon of raw cocoa powder

1 Tablespoon of cocoa nibs (optional)

Mix and roll into balls and put chopped nuts on top if desired.

Place in the freezer for 30 minutes for a more solid texture.

Berry Crumble

1 cup gluten free oats

1 Tablespoon coconut sugar

1 teaspoon vanilla

1/2 cup of chopped nuts

2 Tablespoons of chia seeds

2 Tablespoons coconut oil melted or plant based butter

Drizzle of maple syrup if you wish

Fill your pie dish with organic, fresh or frozen berries of your choice

Mix listed ingredients together and pour on top of the fruit

Bake at 350 degrees (depending your oven heat) for 20-25 minutes

This can be eaten for breakfast or a dessert! *YUM!*

Five Ingredient Cookies!

2 Mashed Bananas

2 Tablespoons of maple syrup or agave
  (We always use a bit less as we both do not like things to be super sweet)

1 cup of GF oats

1/2 cup of tahini (can use peanut butter or almond butter instead)

Vegan chocolate chips for taste

Cook them for ten minutes at 350 degrees, or until they are golden brown.

Be sure not to over bake.

Baked Apples

4 apples

1 teaspoon of cinnamon

1/4 cup of plant butter or 1/4 cup of organic orange juice

Optional: Plant based vanilla or plain yogurt

Slice 4 apples into eighths

Line the pan with plant based melted butter or organic orange juice

Drizzle 1 teaspoon of cinnamon on top

Place in the oven for 15 minutes or until apples are soft

Garnish with plant based plain or vanilla yogurt, and cinnamon.

Chocolate Mug Cake

1 scoop of your favorite vegan chocolate protein powder

1 teaspoon soaked chia

1 Tablespoon coconut flour

1 teaspoon baking powder

1 Tablespoon raw cacao powder

1 Tablespoon chocolate chips

1 flax egg or 4 TBS of aquafaba

2-3 Tablespoons of plant based milk

Mix everything together in the mug, the consistency should be like cake batter

Place in microwave for 45 seconds to 1 min max, the center will be gooey like a lava cake.

Add a dollop of banana plant powered ice cream, vanilla plant based yogurt, raspberries, strawberries or cherries on top.

It's the best EVER!

See page XX for Flax Egg/Aquafaba

Banana plant powered Ice Cream

1 ripe banana per serving

Optional: Cocoa, other fruit*

Peel banana, cut into four sections and freeze banana in plastic bag

Remove from the freezer

Let it sit for 2-5 minutes

Place in the blender or Cuisinart and blend until its ice cream consistency

**Add in cocoa to make chocolate banana plant powered ice cream,
 or fruit to make it a sorbet. Mix everything together.*

Enjoy immediately.

Chocolate Pudding

1/2 cup of cocoa powder

1 teaspoon of vanilla extract

1/2 cup dairy-free milk

1/4 cup pure maple syrup

2 Avocados

Optional:

Plant based yogurt

Raspberries

Bananas

Your choice of nuts

Mix all together in the Cuisinart or nutribullet until it is pudding consistency.

Place in a lovely bowl. We like to layer pudding and then cut banana.

Top with raspberries, bananas, your choice of nuts and your favorite plant based yogurt. We prefer plain.

This takes less than ten minutes to create and is an incredibly delicious and decadent dessert.

"Rule of thumb:
keep it simple,
keep it real, and
keep it fun!"

Tips for Egg replacements

FLAX EGG

Grind flax seed(we use a coffee grinder)

Equal amounts of ground flax seed meal and water make a great egg replacement

Let it gel for ten minutes and it will add structure to any recipe

1 Tablespoon of flax egg equals one regular egg

AQUAFABA

Aquafaba is the liquid from beans and another great egg replacement. Organic garbanzo beans from a can are the easiest to use and our personal favorite.

When shaken up or whisked it has the same consistency as egg whites. It can even be an egg replacement in meringue recipes!

Drain the bean water from the garbanzo beans

Set the garbanzo beans aside to use for something else

Pour the bean water into a mason jar with a tight lid

Shake until frothy

4 Tablespoons of aquafaba equal one regular egg

Cathy and Tricia Brooks

As a mother/daughter team we love creating simple, nutrient dense meals and snacks. We all have such busy lives and without our health we cannot be there for the ones we love, including ourselves. We hope this gives you some inspiration to have fun while preparing healthy meals.

To your happiest and healthiest self!
XO

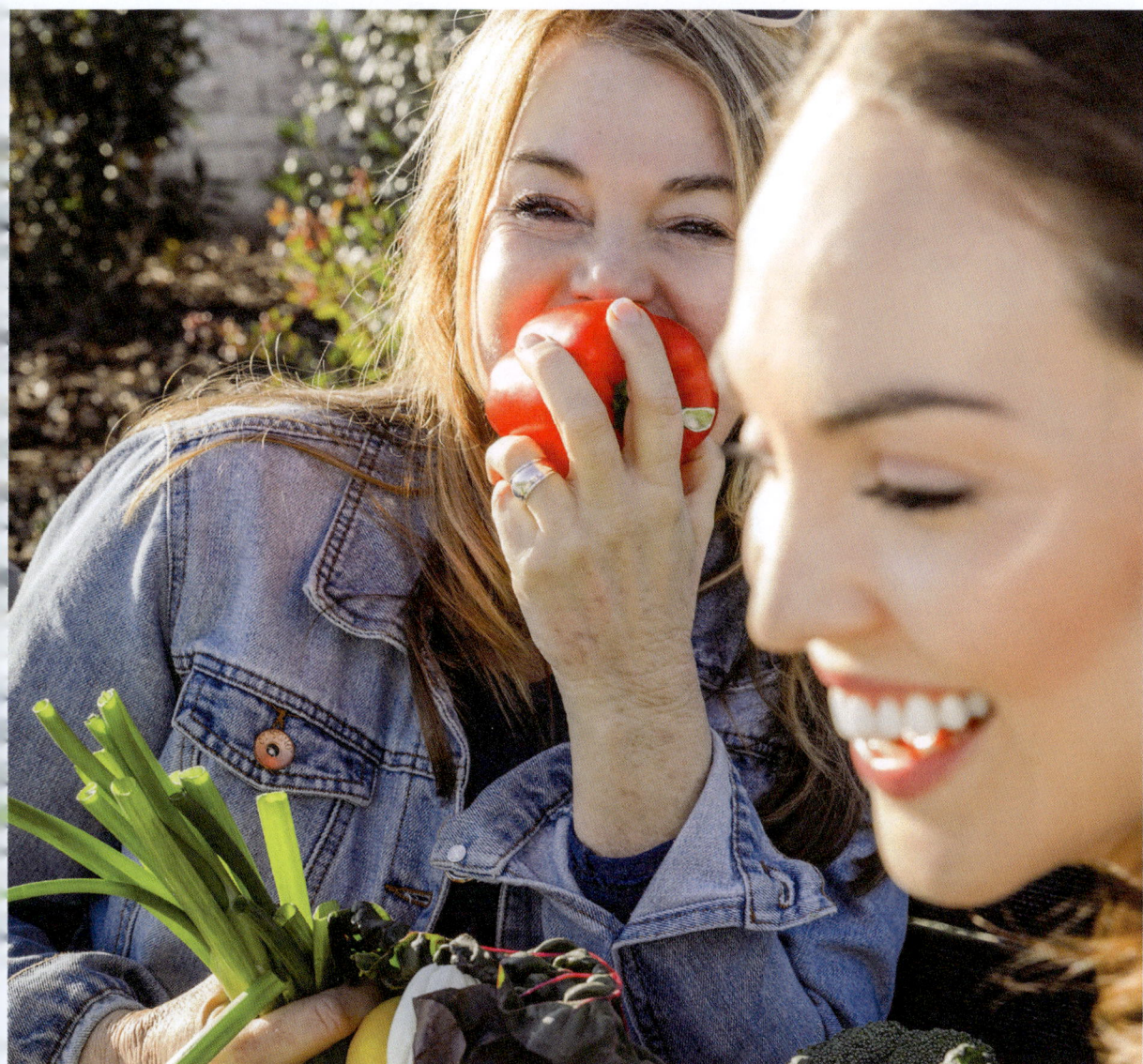

We appreciate you!

Editing/tasting/biggest cheerleader - William Brooks

Photos by Francisco Infante

Graphic design by Darcie Robinson

Contact the Authors

Cathy and Tricia

happiestandhealthiestyou@gmail.com

Volume 1

Printed in Great Britain
by Amazon

82382205R00025